BATS

FLYING FOX BATS

Pamela J. Gerholdt
ABDO & Daughters

Published by Abdo & Daughters, 4940 Viking Drive, Suite 622, Edina, Minnesota 55435.

Library bound edition distributed by Rockbottom Books, Pentagon Tower, P.O. Box 36036, Minneapolis, Minnesota 55435.

Printed in the United States.

Cover Photo credit: Merlin D. Tuttle, Bat Conservation International
Interior Photo credits: Merlin D. Tuttle, Bat Conservation International
Animals, Animals page 5, 21

Edited by Julie Berg

Gerholdt, Pamela J.
   Flying fox bat / Pamela J. Gerholdt.
      p.   cm. — (Bats)
Includes bibliographical references (p. 23) and index.
   ISBN 1-56239-503-3
l. Flying foxes—Juvenile literature. [l. Flying foxes. 2. Bats.] I. Title. II.
Series Gerholdt, Pamela J. Bats.
QL737.C575G48 1995
599.4—dc20   95-7056
                                                                  CIP
                                                                  AC

About The Author

Pam Gerholdt has had a lifelong interest in animals. She is a member of the Minnesota Herpetological Society and is active in conservation issues. She lives in Webster, Minnesota with her husband, sons, and assorted other animals.

Contents

FLYING FOX BATS

There are over 900 **species** of bats in the world. Because they are found in Asia, flying foxes are classified as members of the "Old World" fruit bat family. They have thick fur on their heads and bodies that is grayish brown or black. The fur between their shoulders is often yellow or grayish yellow. As the name suggests, flying foxes look like foxes.

All bats are **mammals**, like dogs, cats, horses, and humans. But bats do something no other mammal can do—they can fly!

The flying fox has long, slender wings that can wrap completely around its body.

WHERE THEY'RE FOUND

Bats live on all of the world's **continents** except Antarctica, the **polar regions**, and a few ocean islands. Flying foxes live in Pakistan, India, Nepal, Sikkim, Bhutan, Burma, Sri Lanka, and the Maldive Islands in the Indian Ocean.

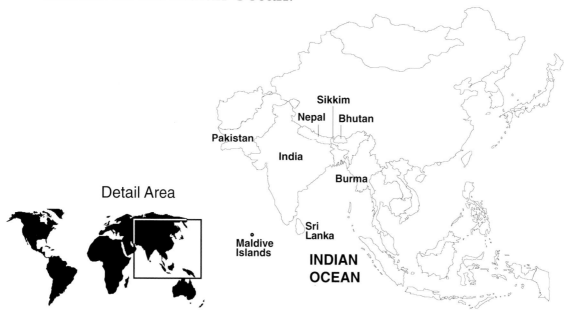

Detail Area

Sikkim
Nepal | Bhutan
Pakistan
India
Burma
Sri Lanka
Maldive Islands

INDIAN OCEAN

A large group of flying fox bats swarming a roost area on an Indian Ocean island.

WHERE THEY LIVE

Flying foxes live in forests, swamps, and on small coastal islands. They **roost** in large groups during the day, usually in trees. Five hundred flying foxes are reported to have roosted in the same **Banyan** tree in India for over 80 years!

These bats do a lot of flapping about and squawking at each other on their roosts. Bats roost by hanging upside down by their feet. It's easy for them because they have 5 toes with sharp, curved claws, and knees that point backwards!

Flying fox bats like to roost in large groups, usually in trees.

SIZES

Flying foxes can grow to over 16 inches (40 cm) long and weigh about 2 to 3.5 pounds (900 to 1,600 g). Their **wing span** is over 5.5 feet (165 cm)! However, most bats are small, 3 to 5 inches (7.5 to 12.5 cm) long and weigh 1 to 3.5 ounces (28 to 98 g).

Some bats are very tiny, like the Kitti's hog-nosed bats, that only grow to 1 inch (2.5 cm) long—about the size of a large bumble bee! Although their body is small, their wing span is 6.5 inches (16.25 cm).

A flying fox bat in flight. Notice its extended wing span.

SHAPES

Everything about flying foxes is LARGE. They have large heads that look like a fox's head with large ears and a long, pointed snout. They have large eyes and can see well.

Most bats have short tails. A few, like the rat-tailed bats, have long tails. But flying foxes don't have tails! They have long, wide wings and are strong fliers.

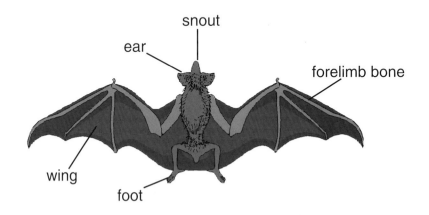

The head of the flying fox bat resembles that of a fox.
It has large ears and a long, pointed snout.

Bats' wings are made of their extra long fingers and **forelimb** bones that support thin, **elastic membranes**. Two membranes, top and bottom, are sandwiched together over the bones on each wing.

SENSES

Flying foxes have the same five senses as humans. Over half of all bat **species** use **echolocation** to "see" in the dark with sound waves. Flying foxes do not use echolocation. They find their food, **roosting** sites, and other bats by looking and listening.

HOW ECHOLOCATION WORKS

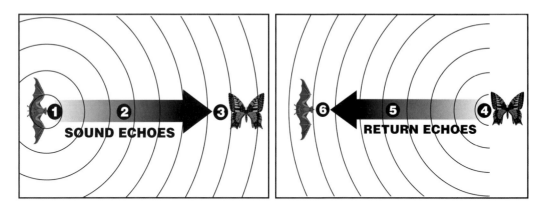

The bat sends out sound echoes (1). These echoes travel in all directions through the air (2). The sound echoes reach an object in the bat's path (3), then bounce off it (4). The return echoes travel through the air (5) and reach the bat (6). These echoes let the bat know where the object is, how large it is, and how fast it is moving.

Flying fox bats don't use echolocation like other bats. They find food with their keen eyesight and hearing.

DEFENSE

Though flying foxes are large, many **predators** consider them "bite-sized." Cats, dogs, raccoons, and skunks eat bats. So do owls, hawks, falcons, snakes and large frogs. Large spiders eat bats that get caught in their webs. Even worse, some bats eat bats! The bat's best defense is to fly away.

Like most bats, flying foxes are **nocturnal**. That means they fly at night, avoiding many predators that hunt by day. Most bats find safe, dark places to hide during the day when they **roost**. But flying foxes will roost in the top branches of trees and are active and noisy as they roost.

For safety, flying fox bats like to roost in tree tops.

FOOD

Flying foxes feed mainly on fruit juices they get from squeezing fruit **pulp** in their mouths. They swallow the juice and spit out the pulp and seeds. If the pulp is very soft, like banana, they will swallow some.

Flying foxes will spend several hours at feeding trees—eating and resting. In some areas they have damaged or ruined fruit **plantations** because they eat so much fruit. Flying foxes will travel 7 to 8.5 miles (12 to 14 km) each night just to find food.

A flying fox bat feeding on a guava.

BABIES

Flying foxes will **breed** twice a year. They have one baby in the spring and another during the **monsoon** season.

Baby bats are very big when they are born. They often weigh 25 percent of their mother's weight. Mother bats take good care of their babies.

Since bats fly, most people think bats are birds that lay eggs. But bats are **mammals**. Their babies are born live.

Baby bats are very large when they are born.

GLOSSARY

BANYON - An East Indian tree of the mulberry family.

BREED - To produce young; also, a kind or type.

CONTINENT (KAHN-tih-nent) - One of the 7 main land masses: Europe, Asia, Africa, North America, South America, Australia and Antarctica.

ECHOLOCATION (ek-o-lo-KAY-shun) - The use of sound waves to find objects.

ELASTIC (ee-LAS-tik) - Able to return to its normal shape after being stretched or bent.

FORELIMB - A front limb of an animal.

MAMMALS (MAM-elz) - Animals with backbones that nurse their young.

MEMBRANES (MEM-branz) - Thin, easily bent layers of animal tissue.

MONSOON - The season during which the wind of the Indian Ocean blows from the southwest, often with heavy rains.

NOCTURNAL (nok-TUR-nul) - Active by night.

PLANTATIONS (plan-TAY-shunz) - Groups of planted trees or plants.

POLAR REGION - Of or near the North or South Pole.

PREDATOR (PRED-uh-tor) - An animal that eats other animals.

PULP - The soft, juicy part of a fruit that is eaten.

ROOST - A place, such as a cave or tree, where bats rest during the day; also, to perch.

SNOUT - The nose and jaws of an animal.

SPECIES (SPEE-seas) - A kind or type.

WING SPAN - The distance from the tip of one outstretched wing to the other.

BIBLIOGRAPHY

Fenton, M. Brock. *Bats.* Facts On File, Inc., 1992.

Findley, James S. *Bats, A Community Perspective.* Cambridge University Press, 1993.

Johnson, Sylvia A. *The World Of Bats.* Lerner Publications Company, 1985.

Nowak, Ronald M. *Walker's Bats Of The World.* The Johns Hopkins University Press, 1994.

Index

DATE DUE
